بسم الله الرحمن الرحيم

refuge

Maryam Bargit

introduction:

Assalamu alaikum warahmatullahi wabarakatuh,
May the peace, mercy and blessings of the Almighty be upon you.

Refuge is a collection of poems I have complied together that deals with heartache and survival through a method of reconnecting with and strengthening one's faith.

I have formulated *Refuge* into a structured emotional journey for readers, characterised by the five chapters which section out its content. The first, being 'on anger and pain' aims to reiterate the concept that is typically embodied by victims or witnesses of hurt or injustice (in the case that 'anger' precedes the notion of 'pain'). The next chapter strives to combat these issues, by focussing 'on patience and hope'. Patience, as an image per se, is seen as a fundamental virtue required for humans to exercise in order to endure hardships and effectively pain. Notably, the theme of patience has been highlighted in the Qur'an through various verses narrating, 'seek assistance by patience and prayer' for 'Allah is certainly with the patient ones.' (2:153) Eventually, by practising such patience, the prospect of hope is brought to life.

This construct is repeated through the following chapter 'on loss and time', where losing something valuable is intrinsically linked to the abstract foundation of time throughout the whole process of healing, and thus, is further highlighted in the succeeding chapter 'on love and gratitude', wherein the method of coping with such loss is depicted through the support of close relations, and most significantly, one's Lord.

Finally, the closing section, 'on the beauty of our creator' extends beyond admiration for our Creator to a level of praise that, as much as I have attempted to express, is always and will always be unequal to His glory and the realism of His favours.

Maryam

Copyright © 2020 by Maryam Bargit

All rights reserved. No part of this book may be reproduced or used in any manner without permission of the copyright owner except for the use of quotations in a book review.

Cover design: Faatima Saiyed

Illustrations: Fowziyah Adam

Calligraphy: Amina Bargit

ISBN: 979-8-6395-6042-2

To Jumainah,

for keeping me anchored

to my motivation,

and to my parents,

for just being you.

table of contents:

on anger and pain

humanity

blood soaked land

ghost town

foolish

weak

on patience and hope

hope

forgiveness

natural process

kite

lesson

rainbow

sunflowers

coping

the Restorer

lost

on loss and time
to my nana
long gone
see you in the small things
years
alone
late
regret

on love and gratitude
beauty
homesick
to my parents
mothers
thank you
grateful

on the beauty of our creator
awe
universe
Him
greater power
journey of a lifetime

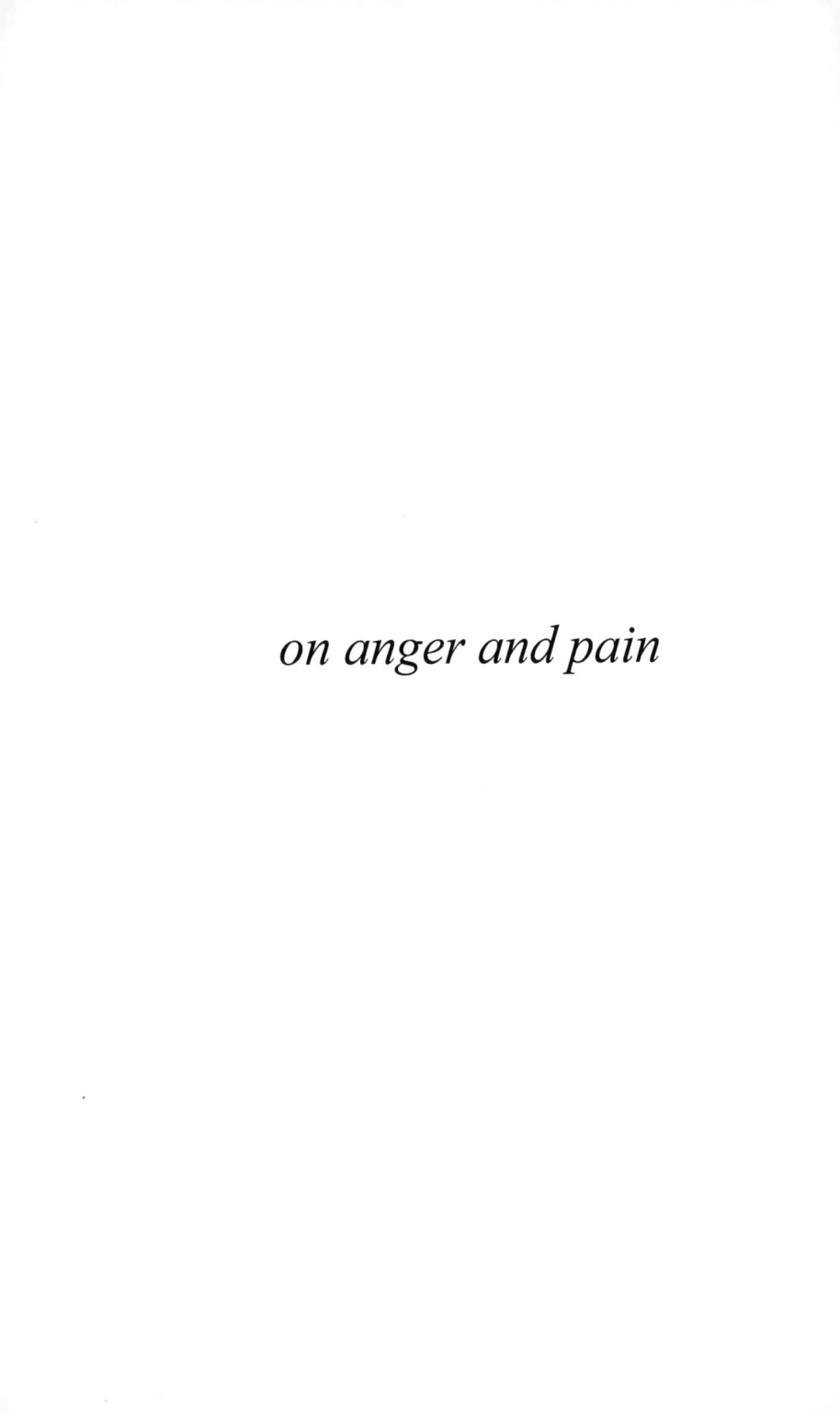

on anger and pain

on anger and pain

humanity

are we just going to sit back and watch

humanity being butchered?

a wife's scream as

her fingers grasp onto her husband's body,

clutching onto his bleeding heart,

served as a metaphor for her own,

watch his life slip between her fingers

like grains of sand and fine dust,

a child's torture as

their house is consumed by a fury of flames- a wildfire,

timber and brick and plaster belched out

within a matter of seconds,

are we just going to turn a blind eye and ignore?

as they are stuck

watching helplessly.

refuge

blood soaked land

a soaring barrage of bullets

rips through the charcoal horizon,

tears through thick tendons of human bones,

ravages its way across homes and

neighbourhoods-

where the distant, nostalgic, hopeful joy

of a child's laughter is

devoured,

it spits out a chewed-up matter of burnt muscle,

and flesh, and limbs,

this state is choked with shards of despair,

despair.

- our people remain indifferent.

on anger and pain

ghost town

guide me through this ghost town,

we can glide like ghosts

submerged into melting melodies of silence

dripping, pouring, gushing

through an empty, blank shell of

what once was.

meander with me through

barren meadows and forgotten trails,

thickening vines and a child's footprint

drifting away into nothingness,

watch this city with me,

fade away like dead wood

of a tree branch excavated

into swirling flames of ash

before our very eyes.

- let us not speak again about this city of bones.

foolish

i told the Almighty about you,

how you stormed into my life like a hurricane

buried a volcano between my ribs

watched it erupt

engulf my entire frame

left me breathless,

alone.

how foolish was i to blind myself to what I had all this time?

for if there is anyone that will listen, it's Him.

on anger and pain

weak

your muffled cries turn into wails

like ships with no sails,

these agonising thoughts

are like torn boats

in a wintry storm

they begin to perfectly form

everyday

like a norm.

you must stand in front of them all,

they mockingly call,

you are not

proud,

confident,

tall,

you are afraid to fall.

on patience and hope

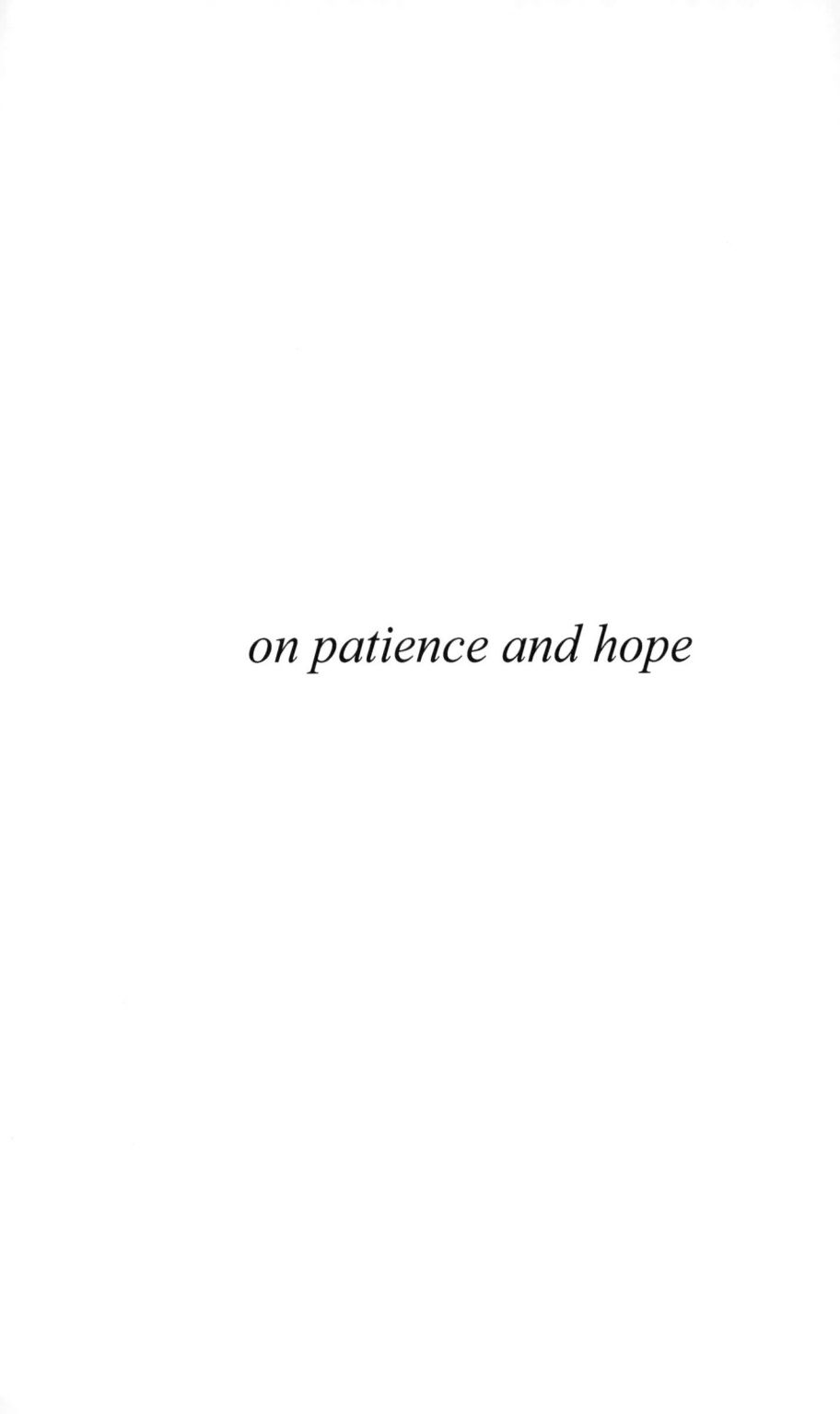

on patience and hope

hope

hope came to me in the form of a dream,

knocked down the bricks of my fortress

invited courage into my chambers

planted seeds of itself along

my ribcage,

watered them every night.

instructed,

"grow, my dear,

there is nothing for you to fear."

forgiveness

"it's putting together the fragments of a shattered mirror
like a jigsaw puzzle,
never knowing if it will ever be complete."

- forgiveness visited me

forgiveness

yanked the knife of betrayal out of my wounds,

-its pain spread like a poisonous wildfire,

buried flaming cannons of rage into

the very depths of my being,

planted itself beneath blackening membranes,

like an unwanted appendage-

forgiveness

undid the knot stuck in my throat,

forgiveness

engulfed the crimson flames of my temper,

on patience and hope

forgiveness

singed flickering embers of my wrath,

forgiveness

obliterated every ounce of my anger,

forgiveness

scorched the trails of my fury,

forgiveness

unshackled my torment from its cage,

and

restored peace from rage.

natural process

i'm struggling to see

through these blurry lines

and twisted kites,

dreams shape shifting into reality

mountains moving into place,

i'm struggling to keep up

with the pace of growth,

the rhythm of life,

the drum of fear,

i need to

s t o p

embrace the present

perpetuate goodness.

on patience and hope

kite

fly your kite

high in the sky,

vibrant yellows and reds

somersaulting -

sailing across entire civilisations

and whole universes,

breathe it out into existence

- your wings were never clipped.

refuge

lesson

they say i can never change lives with stanzas,

but

i have

lived a thousand lives

tucked away into the crevices of my mind

torn from withered pages of borrowed

library books.

i have

dreamed a thousand dreams

buried amongst lost visions in the very crooks of my

existence.

i have

learnt a thousand lessons:

to inspire contents,

move mountains

and fly high.

on patience and hope

rainbow

capture shades of the rainbow,

share its iridescent warmth,

consume folds of darkness

illuminate space between the sky and starlit sea,

follow lost roads to pave tracks across derelict lands,

and

like a dandelion in the breeze

set strings of wishes free from crammed pockets of your

imagination,

grow.

sunflowers

sunflowers blossom from my lungs,

wind through my neck,

stretch out into my mind,

they teach me to rise

after my falls,

stand tall

against the darkness,

never look back at my shadows,

for sunflowers still grow at night.

on patience and hope

coping

for the string of fleeting moments when you

can't help but doubt yourself,

for the days that cloud your vision with torrents of tears,

for the months where you struggle to see beyond your

fears,

for the moments where you have lost your way

struggle to continue with your day,

when things become unclear,

just take a breath and remember,

the light of the Qur'an is always near.

refuge

الْجَبَّارُ

the Restorer

when the tedious d-d-drum of your heart

thrumming beneath your ribcage

consumes your entire being,

when the pounding echo in your head; its

decibels reverberate and weave against each other,

conspire to reach a point of dizziness that slams through you,

when the sight of your shadow grows as dark as charcoal,

when the weight of the universe hangs precariously on your

shoulders

crushes diamonds into misaligned stars,

dispersed across the night sky, like scattered pieces of your

shattered heart,

turn to your Lord,

for no matter the lengths this world takes to tear you apart,

He can always put you back together.

on patience and hope

lost

she was lost

in every possible sense,

stuck at a crossroad

she struggled to see beyond,

arrows pointing in different directions unknown to her,

she felt like a traveller amongst desolate lands,

yet the space around her was filled with people, buildings and nations.

life was an endless cycle she couldn't break out of,

drowning in rain that never stopped pouring,

the path only grew rougher, tougher,

she was addicted,

addicted to these countries fashioned out of gold,

billboards selling the land of false dreams, full of lies and deceit,

persuaded to gamble with her soul,

she was spiralling out of control,

refuge

brimming with shame, fear and despair,

nobody to be held answerable,

could only speak her existence out into

questions of mono syllables,

why, why me?

why?

though she couldn't control her mind flowing back to better days,

when life was dictated by sunny spells and simpler ways,

she remembered,

the interspaces of her youth blossomed with verses

flowing seamlessly past her lips,

distinctly discern letters,

alif,

laam,

meem,

she remembered,

holding The Book lovingly across her chest,

the withered, worn, loved pages of that Book,

on patience and hope

words of a nature so remarkable they spoke out to her,

she remembered,

mindlessly reading words she never really understood,

but in essence, she felt touched, understood,

how if the world were to unite,

not a single letter could be created in its image or like,

she looked towards her shelf,

perched on it, buried in layers of dust

sat that exact same Book,

pages yellowing with antiquity,

she held it in her hands guiltily,

opened a page blindly

and read with ease,

consumed with peace,

she lifted the veil from her heart, she prayed:

"Then with difficulty there certainly is ease,

With difficulty, there certainly is ease." *(30:94)*

on loss and time

on loss and time

to my nana

>you are present in every empty thought,
>
>every trip down memory lane,
>
>the days you stood outside the school yard
>
>even when it began to rain,

>how you unknowingly fed the world around you,
>
>be it through a slice of cake,
>
>the months and years of shopping trips
>
>you took for our own sake,

>your silence lives through unspoken words,
>
>through the cases of visions blurred,
>
>your rare, priceless smile exists
>
>in every second of our glee
>
>every memorabilia and memory
>
>held between you and me,

refuge

where the miles you took stretched into marathons of kindness,
graced your face with a special fondness
merely our happiness was sufficient for such pain
with nothing for you to have gained.

i miss you,
every Saturday at twelve in the afternoon
returning from your shopping trips with all the goods you had bought,
every Thursday visit to replenish our endless stock in fear that it would finish,
catching your trips to the mosque, head bent down low,
every humble comment and the strength you embodied,

i will miss you,
at every joyous occasion
every momentous celebration
at the time of every single prayer
for eternity

on loss and time

for every sacrifice you made on our behalf,
for all the supplications from dawn until dusk
for all the days you opened the doors of Allah's house,
irrespective of the weather.

now, as i stare at everything surrounding me,

orange juice, bananas and boxes of cut-up fruit,

mangos, kiwi, watermelon, grapes- fruit from every season,

twix bars, cupcakes, nuts and food we had never thought existed,

ribena, biscuits, sweets, a list that is forever inexhaustive,

the drawer full of magnum, in the freezer i told you i'd finish one day,

stationery supplies for life

photocopies of every document

just in case

i pray the Almighty grants you
beyond everything you gave us.

Aameen

long gone

you are long gone

but i still see your name sprawled along the walls

beneath layers of chipped paint,

you are long gone

but i still hear echoes of your voice ricocheting in the

silence you left behind,

you are long gone

but i still feel the warmth of your smile in the

brightness of the sunlight,

you are long gone

but i still see the twinkle of your eyes reflected in the stars,

you are long gone

i can't let go of you.

you are long gone

still, you remain.

on loss and time

see you in the small things

i've started waking up early enough

to catch the colour of your

eyes

in the

sunrise,

yellow, pink,

amber,

watch the hues

across the sky

wander,

wonder if the harmony of your voice

could be discerned through whispers of the wind,

rejoice.

years

the years have passed by,

like when the moon pulls the tide in

and the shore struggles to contain itself,

eroded away over a matter of seconds,

unexpectedly and suddenly.

on loss and time

alone

it wasn't until you left,

slamming the door

s h u t .

i realised:

my house could never be a home

without you.

i looked towards the stars in the sky,

to find the trace of your footsteps amongst

them,

i realised:

you'd been lost to me for too long,

i could not recognise what you had become,

for how long?

refuge

late

it's
getting late.
the clock is ticking,
that constant clicking
the sun setting, everyone's
forgetting, before you know the
sun is rising. it's all become so unsurprising

                    r   l
                    e   e
                    p   e
    e   e   p
      a   t
        t   i   w
                    t   a
                    i   k
                    v   e
                    e

cycle of time passing, of dashing off, an unbeatable race against the clock. tick tock, lost, confused.
we fail to see the success we so earnestly search for.
    - it calls for us five times a day.

on loss and time

regret

before it was too late

i wanted to travel the world,

to live a thousand lives,

now i have become lost in the ghost

of maps i used to draw on scrap

pieces of paper,

i wish i chased the clouds of my dreams

to the thoughts in my mind,

much sooner,

before it was too late.

on love and gratitude

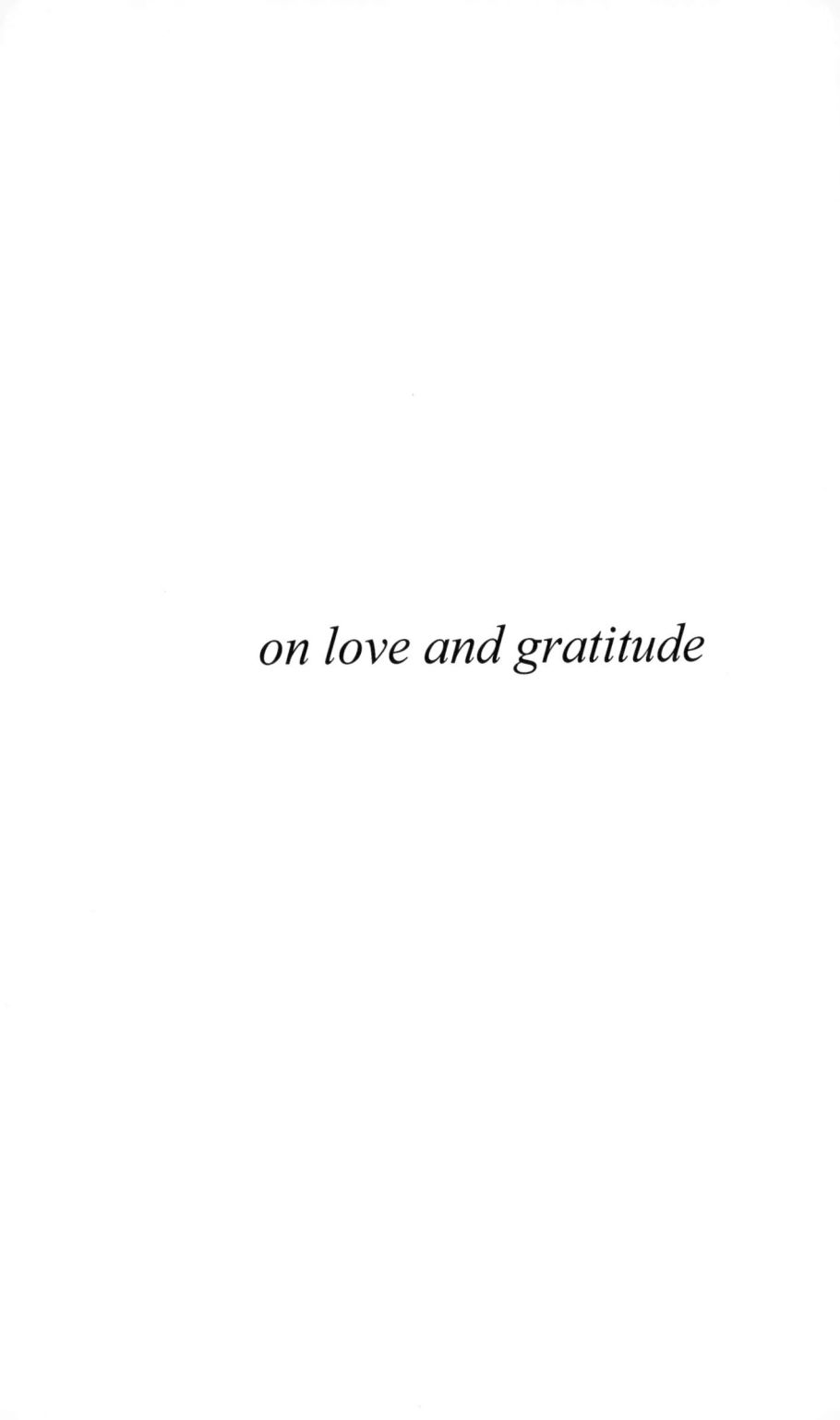

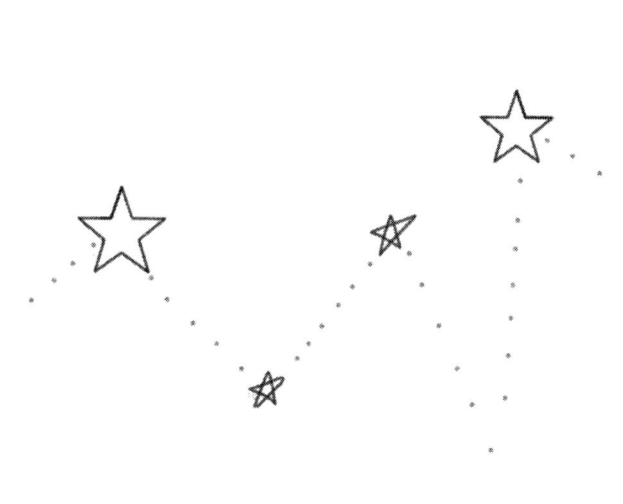

on love and gratitude

beauty

shut your eyes,

conjure up the

sight of

glowing fireflies at twilight

dancing to the symphonies

of birdsong,

a tentative butterfly emerging from its chrysalis

fluttering across a burning horizon,

feel the calm, fresh breeze of a winter morning

stream through cords of your veins,

close your eyes, shape it all into existence.

refuge

homesick

i am homesick

for a place i have never known,

only a glimpse summoned in dreams of my

imagination.

i long to fill vessels from rivers of honey and musk,

bathe under the shade of a bough fashioned out of gold,

perch upon pearls, emeralds, diamonds,

to run freely through fields of saffron,

enclosed into the comforting brightness of light,

teased by a fragrant breeze that

clings to the silky material of

my clothes,

on love and gratitude

encompassed in all its grandeur,

never having the full capacity to picture all of its wonders,

with its splendour multiplied tenfold,

i am stuck,

spluttering on choked consonants

searching for consolation,

desperate, **desperate,** *desperate,*

for such a place

to call home.

refuge

to my parents

there are galaxies in your eyes

brightened by the sparkle of the stars,

there are pathways and motorways,

trace maps along the creases of your hands,

there is a kaleidoscope of colour interlaced within your

irises

casting hope upon the angry, despaired, lost

there is cascading light exuding from the roots of your hair,

flowing steadily along an endless weeping waterfall,

yet

there remains the darkness of a thousand burdens

weaved within the fibres of your muscles.

on love and gratitude

mothers

you taught me to follow roadmaps to the clouds,

dream beyond my imagination,

you've taught me to let the stars dance against my skin,

take each second, hour, time as it passes by,

you've helped me to embrace who i am,

combed through stubborn constellations

flowing down my hair,

believed in me when nobody else did,

wiped away *tsunamis*,

and for you,

i am so grateful.

thank you

your words were the water

to the seeds in our brains

whose stalks grew proudly

through flesh and veins

like sunflowers in the darkness

remaining strong through the emptiness

your words uprooted weeds

and

diffused motivation to the leaves.

on love and gratitude

grateful

i am grateful for

all the rainy days that

washed away my tears,

all the

difficult situations that

forced me to face my fears,

i am grateful for

every bad day when

things didn't go my way,

every yellow that has gone grey,

for all these obstacles served as reminders:

i'm still alive,

i'm still breathing,

that is enough.

on the beauty of our creator

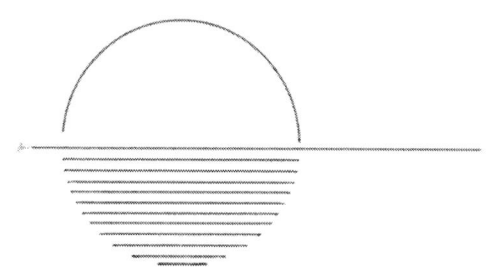

on the beauty of our creator

awe

i wonder when you will stop letting yourself be blinded

from the

beauty of the one who created you,

when it lies right in front of us,

don't you see the simplicity of the smallest sub-atomic

particles

hidden beyond our sight

to the complexities of the galaxies that lay beyond our

reach?

aren't you amazed by the miniscule details etched into your

skin?

a freckle here and a birthmark there,

in awe of your own regular abilities?

universe

there's a whole universe inside of us

made of stardust and clay,

dust and mist somehow entwined to form nebulas of an

organ,

cosmic rays exploding from supernovas,

building celestial realms of capillaries,

there's a whole universe inside of us,

catapulting particles of our existence into perpetual motion,

reversing graveyards of cells

blasting stars across blackened horizons like oxygen traversing

through space.

on the beauty of our creator

Him

unravel the taut bandages

from around your fragile heart

and kneel in front of your Lord,

let Him heal the wounds that adorn

your beating muscle

and

elicit peace from the depths of your soul.

refuge

greater power

she learnt to swim rivers

but they cascaded out

into oceans unknown to

her, lapping against the

sides of her waist,

- she struggles

                                  she learnt to climb hills

                                  but they rolled out into

                                  mountains before her,

                                  towering over her small

                                  figure

                                  - she falls

she's just a little girl in a great big world, too weak to fight and too naive to know, little do you think, she rises after sink with the belief of a greater power who guides her through it all.

on the beauty of our creator

the journey of a lifetime

how i long to gaze at the *Ka'bah*

in awe and wonder

catch sight of it for the first time once again

in all its beauty,

sunlight reflecting off of the *Kiswa* and ponder,

to walk the pathways to *Mina,*

lift my hands in *Arafat*, call out to my Lord,

let my tears form streaks down my cheeks,

soak into my clothes,

how I yearn to lie beneath the starry sky in

Muzdalifah among rows of people,

share smiles and words of encouragement

with fellow pilgrims, pelt the *Jamraat*- the rejected,

to resound the *Labaik* in one voice

stand together in uniform,

as one *ummah*,

one.

you can find me on:
instagram - @poetrybymaryam
twitter - @poetrybymaryam

Acknowledgements:

To everyone who has inspired my every word; teachers, family, friends and strangers.

To Amina, Muhammad, Hafsah, Amira M, Amira G and Khez for all the constant support. Zaynab whose brownies have powered me through compiling this – I'm honestly waiting to win a lifetime supply someday. (Instagram: @zaynabs_delights). My mosque class for the endless amounts of laughter; 'Neeks' for enduring every hurdle in life with me; Mrs Patel (FAP) for believing in me and helping me to achieve my dreams; Amina for the beautiful calligraphy piece; Faatima (Instagram: @createdbyfaatima) and your other half, for bringing realism to my vision; Fowziyah for the amazing illustrations and Jumainah for trusting in my writing from the very first day and conveying an unparalleled amount of assistance and reassurance.

My parents, (the biggest blessing in my life), for pushing me to be the best possible version of myself, for teaching me to reach beyond the stars, for encouraging me, caring for me and advising me.

Finally, may all praise be to the Almighty.

Printed in Great Britain
by Amazon